ONE-TIME GRID

RANDOM PASSWORD BOOK

GRID SERIES
#2

TABLE OF CONTENTS

! IMPORTANT !
HOW TO STORE AND DESTROY THIS BOOK

STORAGE
- Treat this manual with extreme caution when storing. Like any high value item, it's only as safe as the method in which its secured.
- Store out of sight when not in use.
- Do not let others see your storage location.
- Preferably, store in a locked container which cannot be removed from the premises.

DESTRUCTION
- Destroy this manual when at its end-of-life.
- Destruction methods:
    1. Burn its contents completely
    2. Industrial crosscut shredder
    3. Dissolve in an acid solution

ONE-TIME GRID
<u>FACTS</u>

- New One-Time Grid series are generated & published <u>once a week</u>.

- Grids are generated using Python's secure PRNG SystemRandom.

- Enough grids to secure an entire family or network of unique accounts.

- One-Time Grid methods to choose: Random-Grid or Word-Grid

- Random-Grid's use 73 possible characters to populate cells.

- Word-Grid's use a custom corpus of unique and high entropy words with random toggled case.

- Three suggested ways for creating passwords using One-Time Grids.

WHAT MAKES A GOOD PASSWORD?

Size Matters
Create passwords 12 to 21 characters in length, at minimum.

Complexity
Passwords should not be composed solely of common words, names, dates, or numbers.

Non-Sequential
Passwords should not contain sequential numbers or letters: 1234, qwerty, ABCD,…

Unique
Use a different password and creation scheme for every account.

Random Case Changes
Mix uppercase & lowercase characters.

Insert Randomness
Insert random characters and case changes in odd positions throughout the password.

Example Strong Password
Fh&aDa!ptIves0c3

RANDOM CHEAT SHEET
COMMAND LINE RANDOM PASSWORD GENERATION

LINUX/MAC:

```
# openssl rand -base64 20
```
Example)   YnKFUmVPYzQDrK3QT5NZ0Wh51kMBaXw=

```
# date | md5sum  OR # date | md5
```
Example)   c2a505affcd648a3ee9f03c90768bcce

```
# pwgen 10
```
Example)   giepahl3Oy

```
# gpg --gen-random --armor 1 14
```
Example)   1Hs0a5BYKlcRY0wvPy8=

WINDOWS:

```
PS> $Password = ([char[]]([char]33..[char]95) +
([char[]]([char]97..[char]126)) + 0..9 | sort {Get-
Random})[0..8] -join ''
```
Example)   Fj-Rs!4p2z

HOW TO USE
ONE-TIME GRIDS

WHAT IS A "RANDOM-GRID"?

RANDWRD=adaptive   PIN=564068   GRID# 6

	28	27	26	25	24	23	22	
1	D	u	@	V	&	@	(	21
2	F	h	&	s	0	c	3	20
3	h	@	U	p	M	N	M	19
4	C	^	v	0	&	$	8	18
5	T	E	Q	g	R	X	y	17
6	.	*	0	4	0	%	,	16
7	q	r	s	)	4	N	R	15
	8	9	10	11	12	13	14	

Random Grid's are cryptographically random generated 7x7 cells filled with 73 possible characters. They are intented to help you create truly secure random passwords by giving you variable material to use in your password creation.

Also included are **RANDWRD** and **PIN**, each of which are randomly selected and generated. These can be added to a Random Grid password to aid in recall and simplification of your secure password. Learn about the three suggested methods to create passwords using Random Grids.

"BASIC" RANDOM-GRID EXAMPLE

PASSWORD STRENGTH LEVEL = GOOD

RANDWRD=adaptive   PIN=564068   GRID# 6

	28	27	26	25	24	23	22	
1	D	u	@	V	&	@	(	21
2	F	h	&	s	0	c	3	20
3	h	@	U	p	M	N	M	19
4	C	^	v	0	&	$	8	18
5	T	E	Q	g	R	X	y	17
6	•	*	0	4	0	%	,	16
7	q	r	s	)	4	N	R	15
	8	9	10	11	12	13	14	

Step 1: pick two, three, or four random directions to make your password.

@cN$X%N   ,%040*.

Step 2: for added security include RANDWRD or PIN.

@cN$X%N   adaptive   ,%040*.

Step 3: Write down your new account password.

@cN$X%Nadaptive,%040*.

Step 4: Write down your shareable "Grid Key" which corresponds to the Grid# and its outer numbers.

#6 23+R+16

11

"PATTERN" RANDOM-GRID EXAMPLE

PASSWORD STRENGTH LEVEL = EXCELLENT

RANDWRD=adaptive   PIN=564068   GRID# 6

	28	27	26	25	24	23	22	
1	D	u	@	V	&	@	(	21
2	F	h	&	s	0	c	3	20
3	h	@	U	p	M	N	M	19
4	C	^	v	0	&	$	8	18
5	T	E	Q	g	R	X	y	17
6	.	*	0	4	0	%	,	16
7	q	r	s	)	4	N	R	15
	8	9	10	11	12	13	14	

Step 1: pick two, three, or four random patterns to make your password.

&0M&$8   N0gv@F

Step 2: for added security include RANDWRD or PIN.

&0M&$8   564068   N0gv@F   adaptive

Step 3: Write down your new account password.

&0M&$8564068N0gv@Fadaptive

Step 4: Write down your shareable "Grid Key" which corresponds to the Grid# and its outer numbers.

#6 24~18+P+13~2+R

12

"SCATTER" RANDOM-GRID EXAMPLE

PASSWORD STRENGTH LEVEL = EXPERT

RANDWRD=adaptive   PIN=564068   GRID# 6

	28	27	26	25	24	23	22	
1	D	u	@	V	&	@	(	21
2	F	h	&	s	0	c	3	20
3	h	@	U	p	M	N	M	19
4	C	^	v	0	&	$	8	18
5	T	E	Q	g	R	X	y	17
6	.	*	0	4	0	%	,	16
7	q	r	s	)	4	N	R	15
	8	9	10	11	12	13	14	

Step 1: pick 12 to 21 characters at random to make your password.

8u4E.s0FMc0XR@

Step 2: for added security insert the RANDWRD or PIN.

adaptive   8u4E.s0FM   564068   c0XR@

Step 3: Write down your new account password.

adaptive8u4E.s0FM564068c0XR@

WHAT IS A "WORD-GRID"?

	RANDSTR=8cE4TT3	PIN=157683	GRID# 11	
	58	57	56	
1	pRofIles	Pruning	rEgulator	55
2	wAste	tapEstRy	Pointing	54
3	compariSonS	InTerEst	pareNtiNg	53
4	nUTten	harMony	SpEcimen	52
5	wAkiNg	tOpicS	hoMEwork	51
6	rEfilL	tHreeFold	aCceSsoRies	50
7	ascII	infLueNceD	wAsHboard	49
8	....	....	....	48

Words Grid's are cryptographically random selected 3x26 cells filled with unique, high entropy words. They are intended to help you create truly secure random passwords by giving you variable material to use in your password creation.

Also included are **RANDSTR** and **PIN**, each of which are randomly generated. These can be added to a Word Grid password to aid in increasing entropy of your secure password. Learn about the three suggested methods to create passwords using Word Grids.

"BASIC" WORD-GRID EXAMPLE

PASSWORD STRENGTH LEVEL = GOOD

	RANDSTR=8cE4TT3	PIN=157683	GRID# 11	
	58	57	56	
1	pRofIles	Pruning	rEgulator	55
2	wAste	tapEstRy	Pointing	54
3	compariSonS	InTerEst	pareNtiNg	53
4	nUTten	harMony	SpEcimen	52
5	wAkiNg	tOpicS	hoMEwork	51
6	rEfilL	tHreeFold	aCceSsoRies	50
7	ascII	infLueNceD	wAsHboard	49
8	....	....	....	48

Step 1: pick three, four, or five random words in one direction to make your password.
> tOpicS   harMony   InTerEst

Step 2: for added security include RANDSTR or PIN.
> tOpicS   8cE4TT3   harMony   InTerEst

Step 3: Write down your new account password.
> tOpicS8cE4TT3harMonyInTerEst

Step 4: Write down your shareable "Grid Key" which corresponds to the Grid# and its outer numbers.
> #11 57-5+R+4+3

+Step: Not recommended but for ease of recall you could remove the case toggling, for instance:
> topics   harmony   interest

"PATTERN" WORD-GRID EXAMPLE

PASSWORD STRENGTH LEVEL = EXCELLENT

	RANDSTR=8cE4TT3	PIN=157683	GRID# 11	
	58	57	56	
1	pRofIles	Pruning	rEgulator	55
2	wAste	tapEstRy	Pointing	54
3	compariSonS	InTerEst	pareNtiNg	53
4	nUTten	harMony	SpEcimen	52
5	wAkiNg	tOpicS	hoMEwork	51
6	rEfilL	tHreeFold	aCceSsoRies	50
7	ascII	infLueNceD	wAsHboard	49
8	....	....	....	48

Step 1: pick three, four, or five random words in a unique pattern to make your password.

    aCceSsoRies   hoMEwork   tOpicS

Step 2: for added security include RANDSTR or PIN.

    aCceSsoRies   hoMEwork   157683 tOpicS

Step 3: Write down your new account password.

    aCceSsoRieshoMEwork157683tOpicS

Step 4: Write down your shareable "Grid Key" which corresponds to the Grid# and its outer numbers.

    #11 50-51+P-57

+Step: Not recommended but for ease of recall you could remove the case toggling, for instance:

    accessories   homework   topics

"SCATTER" WORD-GRID EXAMPLE

PASSWORD STRENGTH LEVEL = EXPERT

	RANDSTR=8cE4TT3	PIN=157683	GRID# 11	
	58	57	56	
1	pRofIles	Pruning	rEgulator	55
2	wAste	tapEstRy	Pointing	54
3	compariSonS	InTerEst	pareNtiNg	53
4	nUTten	harMony	SpEcimen	52
5	wAkiNg	tOpicS	hoMEwork	51
6	rEfilL	tHreeFold	aCceSsoRies	50
7	ascII	infLueNceD	wAsHboard	49
8	....	....	....	48

Step 1: pick three, four, or five random words to make your password.

harMony pareNtiNg rEfilL compariSonS

Step 2: for added security include RANDSTR or PIN.

harMony8cE4TT3pareNtiNg rEfilL compariSonS

Step 3: Write down your new account password.

harMony8cE4TT3pareNtiNgrEfilLcompariSonS

+Step: Not recommended but for ease of recall you could remove the case toggling, for instance:

harmony parenting refill comparisons

WHAT IS A "GRID KEY"?

SHARE PASSWORDS SECURELY

RANDWRD=adaptive   PIN=564068   GRID# 6

	28	27	26	25	24	23	22	
1	D	u	@	V	&	@	(	21
2	F	h	&	s	0	c	3	20
3	h	@	U	p	M	N	M	19
4	C	^	v	0	&	$	8	18
5	T	E	Q	g	R	X	y	17
6	.	*	0	4	0	%	,	16
7	q	r	s	)	4	N	R	15
	8	9	10	11	12	13	14	

GRID KEYS help describe how a password was created. Grid Keys enable users on the same *Grid Series* to share passwords securely without sending the actual password.

[Grid#]-[Part1]-[Part2]-[Part3]-...
R=RANDWRD P=PIN

Step 1: We pick three parts to make our password.
@cN$X%N   adaptive   ,%040*.

Step 2: Note Grid# & cell #'s that convey direction.
Grid #**6** 23=@cN$X%N R=adaptive 16=,%040*.

Step 3: Assembled our Grid Key equals = 6-23-R-16

Step 4: Now share 6-23-R-16 instead of the password:
@cN$X%Nadaptive,%040*.

MASTER GRID TEMPLATE

RANDWRD=   PIN=   GRID#

	28	27	26	25	24	23	22	
1								21
2								20
3								19
4								18
5								17
6								16
7								15
	8	9	10	11	12	13	14	

Master Grid Template is provided as a way to record
a shared password creation scheme. This enables a
user to highlight the cells above with the custom
pattern and then reference as needed.

One could also record their own custom RANDWRD or
PIN number to use. This gives a user an added layer
of variance from the provided grids.

RANDOM-GRIDS

	28	27	26	25	24	23	22	
1	Q	#	{	4	d	L	3	21
2	w	5	3	:	0	-	9	20
3	]	9	.	8	?	j	8	19
4	M	D	h	C	}	w	P	18
5	n	A	u	{	z	1	Z	17
6	x	b	#	d	o	e	5	16
7	c	R	D	^	%	e	4	15
	8	9	10	11	12	13	14	

	28	27	26	25	24	23	22	
1	[	h	]	r	x	4	t	21
2	%	9	6	q	2	Z	;	20
3	2	0	F	$	9	H	d	19
4	8	1	A	.	N	^	N	18
5	.	#	t	p	)	u	c	17
6	K	O	S	)	w	0	K	16
7	^	4	f	V	E	n	*	15
	8	9	10	11	12	13	14	

	28	27	26	25	24	23	22	
1	e	D	V	O	N	r	2	21
2	k	i	o	F	A	Q	:	20
3	;	u	S	X	K	V	M	19
4	B	,	V	0	#	v	M	18
5	o	m	M	8	$	B	w	17
6	P	H	U	Q	]	#	7	16
7	}	-	v	h	2	(	P	15
	8	9	10	11	12	13	14	

RANDWRD=order   PIN=515592   GRID# 4

	28	27	26	25	24	23	22	
1	f	5	P	0	%	j	S	21
2	M	d	T	N	s	%	9	20
3	H	x	S	(	E	O	u	19
4	q	$	W	{	V	u	r	18
5	1	5	5	6	V	H	V	17
6	p	.	M	(	u	0	Y	16
7	?	3	i	N	E	Y	z	15
	8	9	10	11	12	13	14	

	28	27	26	25	24	23	22	
1	9	:	D	?	$	k	j	21
2	U	6	s	^	g	{	5	20
3	N	E	c	)	T	(	b	19
4	A	Z	L	I	E	L	d	18
5	B	?	X	9	M	?	#	17
6	K	^	0	G	$	%	0	16
7	w	V	3	L	H	O	C	15
	8	9	10	11	12	13	14	

RANDWRD=technician   PIN=593595   GRID# 6

	28	27	26	25	24	23	22	
1	0	N	,	u	@	)	B	21
2	V	d	D	g	j	5	L	20
3	A	f	M	j	5	Z	*	19
4	^	N	o	h	D	a	(	18
5	a	-	c	g	x	k	;	17
6	y	T	I	$	!	;	z	16
7	!	t	e	g	n	l	T	15
	8	9	10	11	12	13	14	

RANDWRD=gathered   PIN=571387   GRID# 7

	28	27	26	25	24	23	22	
1	4	s	Z	H	6	F	0	21
2	9	S	v	b	]	O	d	20
3	H	9	A	W	T	I	g	19
4	t	M	!	V	z	T	7	18
5	!	r	[	a	r	$	^	17
6	a	G	D	r	s	y	I	16
7	?	B	u	U	h	@	!	15
	8	9	10	11	12	13	14	

RANDWRD=coaches   PIN=304789   GRID# 8

	28	27	26	25	24	23	22	
1	-	z	e	I	w	q	C	21
2	Z	s	T	r	D	u	b	20
3	O	Z	e	S	O	B	2	19
4	;	M	w	K	m	s	1	18
5	4	P	F	&	K	c	F	17
6	&	x	Y	0	y	0	M	16
7	j	K	:	S	N	!	f	15
	8	9	10	11	12	13	14	

RANDWRD=stalemate   PIN=147255   GRID# 9

	28	27	26	25	24	23	22	
1	R	e	*	[	#	+	z	21
2	c	J	4	q	&	t	-	20
3	5	!	y	A	S	6	t	19
4	f	v	H	1	5	E	Q	18
5	p	E	P	H	]	I	o	17
6	1	D	S	0	f	X	6	16
7	6	-	@	5	Z	P	u	15
	8	9	10	11	12	13	14	

RANDWRD=eggbeater   PIN=833303   GRID# 10

	28	27	26	25	24	23	22	
1	o	Z	.	x	!	I	$	21
2	p	y	u	,	Z	c	5	20
3	@	]	]	}	*	L	[	19
4	:	I	X	.	d	,	i	18
5	k	}	$	-	1	A	0	17
6	S	}	O	:	s	q	R	16
7	;	7	q	1	u	s	3	15
	8	9	10	11	12	13	14	

	28	27	26	25	24	23	22	
1	4	(	w	y	Y	O	F	21
2	A	9	E	;	s	j	)	20
3	x	7	2	!	!	y	5	19
4	d	1	U	n	P	2	V	18
5	K	.	)	!	S	W	G	17
6	W	i	f	v	j	:	$	16
7	J	V	C	n	]	?	:	15
	8	9	10	11	12	13	14	

	28	27	26	25	24	23	22	
1	T	%	P	-	u	(	L	21
2	Z	J	b	q	N	j	O	20
3	.	@	&	R	Z	t	u	19
4	X	t	,	I	c	;	6	18
5	@	3	X	J	g	I	b	17
6	t	9	?	O	.	E	-	16
7	?	@	}	F	{	A	s	15
	8	9	10	11	12	13	14	

	28	27	26	25	24	23	22	
1	2	C	{	{	B	,	U	21
2	C	)	w	c	7	D	S	20
3	]	Z	^	3	,	z	P	19
4	m	q	8	N	}	7	n	18
5	u	7	^	z	#	)	g	17
6	:	5	W	P	m	3	t	16
7	L	M	@	!	F	I	8	15
	8	9	10	11	12	13	14	

	28	27	26	25	24	23	22	
1	I	}	,	O	v	;	J	21
2	-	[	K	:	g	9	a	20
3	#	g	&	E	@	N	a	19
4	h	?	@	s	)	c	J	18
5	E	^	L	F	c	C	z	17
6	w	m	Z	R	K	R	$	16
7	%	I	J	0	a	.	m	15
	8	9	10	11	12	13	14	

RANDWRD=motors   PIN=004155   GRID# 15

	28	27	26	25	24	23	22	
1	W	C	)	Z	9	I	^	21
2	S	x	3	L	m	:	z	20
3	.	J	d	u	M	%	X	19
4	!	z	0	8	V	D	n	18
5	8	V	3	v	)	+	7	17
6	W	b	x	T	r	q	^	16
7	z	k	)	O	D	Y	@	15
	8	9	10	11	12	13	14	

RANDWRD=cleveland   PIN=445056   GRID# 16

	28	27	26	25	24	23	22	
1	2	K	q	O	8	T	5	21
2	3	N	:	B	u	#	D	20
3	X	1	M	m	%	w	0	19
4	K	;	9	0	B	O	.	18
5	0	n	W	*	[	P	u	17
6	g	C	a	0	P	P	5	16
7	V	V	[	D	T	Z	O	15
	8	9	10	11	12	13	14	

29

RANDWRD=angle   PIN=141923   GRID# 17

	28	27	26	25	24	23	22	
1	G	5	P	r	8	Y	O	21
2	&	m	5	a	9	N	%	20
3	[	,	K	j	B	x	G	19
4	D	z	;	#	%	U	3	18
5	+	+	V	G	0	U	H	17
6	6	j	f	}	V	N	a	16
7	Y	A	J	&	G	#	k	15
	8	9	10	11	12	13	14	

RANDWRD=enduring   PIN=121806   GRID# 18

	28	27	26	25	24	23	22	
1	d	I	t	-	*	o	!	21
2	z	a	m	S	h	f	7	20
3	1	l	{	N	p	*	%	19
4	n	b	x	.	o	S	6	18
5	x	r	&	U	r	L	!	17
6	o	,	#	X	-	8	,	16
7	E	%	C	:	N	g	U	15
	8	9	10	11	12	13	14	

	28	27	26	25	24	23	22	
1	,	A	7	}	w	y	f	21
2	%	d	?	+	]	L	K	20
3	i	h	e	A	K	w	y	19
4	0	G	G	R	]	G	#	18
5	?	W	?	i	D	c	h	17
6	K	C	y	m	y	6	o	16
7	,	q	b	i	N	L	#	15
	8	9	10	11	12	13	14	

	28	27	26	25	24	23	22	
1	u	0	p	S	o	,	U	21
2	*	F	%	)	h	z	:	20
3	&	@	K	S	1	C	:	19
4	B	k	k	H	J	}	A	18
5	R	}	5	]	D	.	,	17
6	.	Z	P	Z	T	+	.	16
7	:	C	j	V	#	}	;	15
	8	9	10	11	12	13	14	

RANDWRD=impressed   PIN=286791   GRID# 21

	28	27	26	25	24	23	22	
1	q	X	z	F	r	s	F	21
2	0	5	9	d	9	[	d	20
3	@	x	o	5	a	H	:	19
4	f	p	t	-	O	0	3	18
5	c	5	F	;	h	@	K	17
6	i	}	M	E	M	]	m	16
7	a	M	c	@	O	x	y	15
	8	9	10	11	12	13	14	

RANDWRD=responded   PIN=506769   GRID# 22

	28	27	26	25	24	23	22	
1	G	q	}	Y	%	O	7	21
2	C	j	N	+	G	d	6	20
3	-	+	N	j	U	4	d	19
4	}	r	H	H	c	n	J	18
5	8	3	o	$	A	Q	q	17
6	4	c	#	0	C	n	j	16
7	G	G	r	s	?	W	F	15
	8	9	10	11	12	13	14	

	28	27	26	25	24	23	22	
1	h	d	d	]	P	L	l	21
2	S	9	Y	s	G	Q	]	20
3	{	I	Y	+	S	^	k	19
4	i	b	q	c	A	E	1	18
5	8	0	1	]	X	]	U	17
6	o	L	z	*	v	1	d	16
7	2	(	(	4	&	4	-	15
	8	9	10	11	12	13	14	

	28	27	26	25	24	23	22	
1	)	i	@	A	-	{	u	21
2	@	G	;	a	R	N	b	20
3	y	@	C	T	4	M	J	19
4	!	Y	s	7	g	2	p	18
5	!	j	$	h	!	@	5	17
6	c	)	k	]	?	x	j	16
7	V	0	b	:	T	1	c	15
	8	9	10	11	12	13	14	

RANDWRD=bring   PIN=792555   GRID# 25

	28	27	26	25	24	23	22	
1	Y	f	z	6	f	8	b	21
2	a	T	)	h	E	]	z	20
3	q	$	&	j	4	S	V	19
4	0	K	w	]	B	8	C	18
5	C	,	O	M	M	V	%	17
6	T	M	5	p	R	v	Z	16
7	p	K	n	d	1	:	K	15
	8	9	10	11	12	13	14	

RANDWRD=canned   PIN=593777   GRID# 26

	28	27	26	25	24	23	22	
1	3	u	:	:	%	0	3	21
2	9	j	n	w	?	g	L	20
3	0	;	C	,	X	9	n	19
4	}	H	[	]	Z	$	W	18
5	i	]	K	w	T	?	A	17
6	U	$	Y	M	w	,	%	16
7	w	(	D	t	7	s	W	15
	8	9	10	11	12	13	14	

34

	28	27	26	25	24	23	22	
1	^	,	*	d	V	@	g	21
2	A	0	*	F	H	D	c	20
3	X	!	V	?	g	;	#	19
4	C	B	1	4	6	:	u	18
5	o	G	L	H	{	d	@	17
6	e	w	T	Q	%	V	p	16
7	N	#	0	&	r	:	3	15
	8	9	10	11	12	13	14	

	28	27	26	25	24	23	22	
1	V	q	B	Z	M	C	e	21
2	-	y	C	n	*	g	w	20
3	n	2	g	X	Y	L	U	19
4	?	F	q	C	u	p	L	18
5	}	t	w	!	0	j	C	17
6	R	J	)	8	0	*	g	16
7	A	V	^	P	G	c	e	15
	8	9	10	11	12	13	14	

RANDWRD=island   PIN=045633   GRID# 29

	28	27	26	25	24	23	22	
1	S	L	P	:	h	w	Q	21
2	z	)	S	$	N	r	R	20
3	4	.	q	a	-	D	V	19
4	Z	v	w	Y	4	8	o	18
5	J	z	I	!	&	G	a	17
6	5	z	8	)	M	f	R	16
7	q	h	p	W	-	z	E	15
	8	9	10	11	12	13	14	

RANDWRD=verse   PIN=854165   GRID# 30

	28	27	26	25	24	23	22	
1	W	0	q	2	G	+	O	21
2	w	4	)	A	3	.	K	20
3	U	5	o	B	8	}	#	19
4	$	x	P	#	t	R	z	18
5	&	?	V	o	x	.	&	17
6	$	m	;	{	)	r	W	16
7	K	t	n	m	6	a	]	15
	8	9	10	11	12	13	14	

36

	28	27	26	25	24	23	22	
1	0	#	}	Z	c	!	U	21
2	A	-	(	J	4	2	a	20
3	w	R	}	U	T	X	Z	19
4	V	4	V	Q	[	F	!	18
5	q	L	G	#	1	c	]	17
6	W	&	I	t	6	1	[	16
7	Y	f	i	@	w	.	W	15
	8	9	10	11	12	13	14	

	28	27	26	25	24	23	22	
1	V	Z	C	+	O	S	+	21
2	T	5	p	;	Z	Y	c	20
3	q	n	3	H	7	4	:	19
4	&	M	8	G	6	6	s	18
5	!	c	^	t	:	U	Q	17
6	N	z	[	!	7	m	C	16
7	E	6	g	V	6	?	{	15
	8	9	10	11	12	13	14	

	28	27	26	25	24	23	22	
1	p	o	q	H	,	,	5	21
2	p	x	i	$	$	O	F	20
3	8	}	}	$	f	v	n	19
4	)	e	:	S	y	6	^	18
5	:	0	}	O	p	B	+	17
6	q	p	0	r	&	&	2	16
7	Q	x	q	!	w	u	A	15
	8	9	10	11	12	13	14	

	28	27	26	25	24	23	22	
1	r	3	C	b	J	Q	i	21
2	[	s	D	d	U	y	r	20
3	l	j	g	P	*	k	8	19
4	s	G	f	y	+	G	{	18
5	a	a	]	+	K	V	E	17
6	?	e	,	s	o	B	o	16
7	G	(	s	V	t	y	U	15
	8	9	10	11	12	13	14	

RANDWRD=slight   PIN=390800   GRID# 35

	28	27	26	25	24	23	22	
1	x	8	q	1	(	A	)	21
2	7	B	%	@	j	B	y	20
3	p	z	(	A	9	B	D	19
4	b	1	M	w	X	P	;	18
5	2	-	h	F	6	C	;	17
6	G	U	4	&	u	-	8	16
7	K	1	!	1	]	X	9	15
	8	9	10	11	12	13	14	

RANDWRD=stumbling   PIN=911198   GRID# 36

	28	27	26	25	24	23	22	
1	?	d	w	(	d	E	z	21
2	?	9	W	Q	0	s	p	20
3	:	Q	+	}	n	F	$	19
4	[	j	+	p	%	d	%	18
5	4	3	0	W	[	w	O	17
6	o	a	S	C	2	:	d	16
7	t	g	;	}	K	o	k	15
	8	9	10	11	12	13	14	

	28	27	26	25	24	23	22	
1	L	O	H	]	-	}	I	21
2	:	&	7	K	Q	o	v	20
3	:	4	k	1	}	3	.	19
4	%	d	@	Q	@	!	r	18
5	9	O	z	b	,	.	r	17
6	a	C	z	T	G	C	w	16
7	i	q	N	T	e	d	Z	15
	8	9	10	11	12	13	14	

	28	27	26	25	24	23	22	
1	(	.	x	J	s	g	2	21
2	K	p	}	S	^	:	Z	20
3	g	5	E	4	8	o	7	19
4	J	O	o	i	S	!	a	18
5	x	e	0	R	r	!	s	17
6	C	i	L	t	E	X	}	16
7	p	4	(	L	D	Q	&	15
	8	9	10	11	12	13	14	

RANDWRD=flavorful PIN=383520 GRID# 39

	28	27	26	25	24	23	22	
1	(	:	{	y	b	m	m	21
2	H	u	0	3	i	f	p	20
3	r	a	-	E	T	}	r	19
4	e	Y	I	g	c	w	$	18
5	G	+	A	,	u	J	(	17
6	@	]	1	R	Y	Q	:	16
7	7	;	H	;	R	*	$	15
	8	9	10	11	12	13	14	

RANDWRD=ottawa PIN=131310 GRID# 40

	28	27	26	25	24	23	22	
1	5	]	.	!	$	Y	,	21
2	o	3	6	t	#	f	I	20
3	f	.	R	b	9	.	S	19
4	g	0	J	c	T	;	P	18
5	}	b	Y	k	{	q	i	17
6	I	E	o	.	2	:	l	16
7	J	d	O	2	N	Y	X	15
	8	9	10	11	12	13	14	

	28	27	26	25	24	23	22	
1	r	1	D	t	z	-	:	21
2	e	e	t	h	]	f	r	20
3	:	#	r	*	n	3	O	19
4	^	K	:	%	F	i	)	18
5	u	{	Z	G	1	j	0	17
6	n	q	A	m	.	f	K	16
7	U	]	f	m	x	D	9	15
	8	9	10	11	12	13	14	

	28	27	26	25	24	23	22	
1	!	6	X	1	$	T	p	21
2	1	F	h	9	K	w	k	20
3	8	7	U	8	I	m	W	19
4	j	#	z	;	#	c	k	18
5	@	a	O	6	I	I	g	17
6	Y	7	O	w	m	d	n	16
7	o	5	b	]	m	W	s	15
	8	9	10	11	12	13	14	

	28	27	26	25	24	23	22	
1	L	d	@	-	Y	@	l	21
2	2	r	*	D	i	H	q	20
3	O	g	Z	F	-	9	s	19
4	,	9	M	0	n	i	Z	18
5	0	f	2	x	-	p	p	17
6	9	J	B	0	4	f	0	16
7	$	i	5	3	1	z	)	15
	8	9	10	11	12	13	14	

	28	27	26	25	24	23	22	
1	n	%	W	B	i	,	D	21
2	x	9	0	+	E	k	9	20
3	{	x	S	N	9	q	2	19
4	2	2	&	m	7	r	v	18
5	B	v	^	-	w	(	I	17
6	S	T	C	p	@	X	0	16
7	v	f	.	-	o	e	d	15
	8	9	10	11	12	13	14	

	28	27	26	25	24	23	22	
1	S	V	%	@	5	H	4	21
2	8	r	f	P	-	L	q	20
3	U	P	N	c	%	T	:	19
4	{	^	M	I	t	1	0	18
5	c	I	z	3	s	!	x	17
6	0	]	H	2	a	)	]	16
7	g	0	@	4	4	^	E	15
	8	9	10	11	12	13	14	

	28	27	26	25	24	23	22	
1	t	r	p	a	A	L	Q	21
2	6	0	G	.	A	z	S	20
3	j	}	D	?	#	F	V	19
4	Y	S	p	D	E	j	o	18
5	7	n	Z	a	1	v	R	17
6	E	6	F	d	f	t	b	16
7	]	T	R	^	L	E	B	15
	8	9	10	11	12	13	14	

RANDWRD=software   PIN=217167   GRID# 47

	28	27	26	25	24	23	22	
1	P	m	V	A	1	k	I	21
2	Y	R	I	X	m	(	W	20
3	)	9	d	-	V	7	6	19
4	h	}	T	U	W	G	9	18
5	^	S	J	(	B	9	s	17
6	#	M	J	1	q	M	0	16
7	W	k	+	f	W	m	2	15
	8	9	10	11	12	13	14	

RANDWRD=expediter   PIN=651496   GRID# 48

	28	27	26	25	24	23	22	
1	K	b	r	t	X	z	0	21
2	a	,	+	s	u	}	R	20
3	I	k	d	C	M	0	g	19
4	W	}	B	@	{	T	)	18
5	H	,	9	z	1	#	N	17
6	)	h	C	6	,	T	.	16
7	$	c	f	q	-	[	L	15
	8	9	10	11	12	13	14	

RANDWRD=adobe   PIN=015542   GRID# 49

	28	27	26	25	24	23	22	
1	o	O	}	Y	,	b	;	21
2	&	P	R	I	m	}	+	20
3	g	Y	U	m	A	0	S	19
4	(	Q	]	H	?	M	r	18
5	Z	j	m	r	5	#	&	17
6	1	f	S	X	H	S	d	16
7	p	!	w	9	J	G	e	15
	8	9	10	11	12	13	14	

RANDWRD=designated   PIN=539744   GRID# 50

	28	27	26	25	24	23	22	
1	A	J	4	!	e	B	@	21
2	u	w	:	8	7	5	e	20
3	^	#	&	q	W	t	0	19
4	0	x	[	x	1	I	5	18
5	K	6	t	9	*	M	*	17
6	*	6	+	f	h	p	2	16
7	d	z	e	?	R	w	}	15
	8	9	10	11	12	13	14	

WORD-GRIDS

	58	57	56	
1	dIscusseD	oxiDE	seneGAl	55
2	SwimmAble	exHibIt	reiTErate	54
3	raIdeR	participANt	TinkeR	53
4	raspinG	reCorDings	Ricky	52
5	metHodolOgy	tournaMeNts	comMunicatE	51
6	dRaIn	Households	wolVeRine	50
7	structuREd	pUnishment	drainpIpE	49
8	prEparatioN	TOmato	circUlar	48
9	suRreNder	staTistIcs	FiltrAte	47
10	tRaIler	eveNtUally	aNgeLfish	46
11	FooTrest	WoRldcat	bReeD	45
12	grEnadA	eastcoAst	Seminar	44
13	unDercOok	seParaTion	TactLess	43
14	daRkness	correlatIoN	BullIsh	42
15	uNwashEd	moderaToR	zaMbIa	41
16	releAseD	cRinkLy	adVances	40
17	celIBacy	fReestyLe	puNCtuate	39
18	AllIance	outhoUse	backgRouNd	38
19	charMS	botTleS	membRane	37
20	verzeichNiS	sUrroGate	cOAster	36
21	cOnduCt	carnIvorE	bacKLess	35
22	SLept	JewiSh	inexpeNsivE	34
23	wOrldS	changeLog	OutSider	33
24	wiEldable	diSTinct	cOndenSe	32
25	vegetatIon	IndeeD	confiNIng	31
26	AnswErs	sPotless	cLothes	30
	27	28	29	

	RANDSTR=xtMI*-S 58	PIN=259542 57	GRID# 2 56	
1	dEmographIc	deCLined	CorrectiOn	55
2	currEnTly	workSTation	deveLopS	54
3	radIAted	dispErSed	POtentially	53
4	reverSIng	poLIsh	traVerSe	52
5	conSISt	busYbodY	iMageS	51
6	ecOLogist	gladLy	extoRtion	50
7	becOmeS	sUpermaN	cOnvicTed	49
8	OutmosT	sCrawnY	cOmmitted	48
9	OccuPancy	delIghT	dImenSions	47
10	dysleXic	rocKlike	TiliNg	46
11	DecadE	baRRette	powDeRy	45
12	teMpOrary	frequEntly	meMories	44
13	sensaTioN	DeteRmines	thrEateN	43
14	puncturED	vocaLizE	raNginG	42
15	entwine	steAdfaSt	dArkisH	41
16	moonRiSe	BacksliD	backYard	40
17	rAspinG	synapSE	iCons	39
18	unguarDed	bUbblE	ExaminiNg	38
19	housEwivEs	landlOrd	cerTaiN	37
20	diFfuSer	BoogeyMan	RespondEnt	36
21	muSclE	BRowbeat	sTimulaTe	35
22	chIrpIng	iMagInary	correlatIon	34
23	banKrOll	cOvEr	EmbarGo	33
24	aCcessiblE	daylIGht	syntheTIc	32
25	pUrifIer	boundINg	childhood	31
26	prostOrEs	lucratIve	comModore	30
	27	28	29	

	58	57	56	
1	descRibinG	cAtnip	WaLker	55
2	VeNding	seTtlinG	pAralyZe	54
3	AnsweRing	robinSoN	HaRvey	53
4	wiLdfoWl	mounTIng	switchED	52
5	RetRy	Housewares	goldmine	51
6	eNglish	TrOpics	talentED	50
7	crEatablE	twidDLe	jAybiRd	49
8	diScretIon	engravEr	trIcKy	48
9	designInG	treatMents	ContrAry	47
10	eNgUlf	bactErIal	uNpInned	46
11	mEtadaTa	firEwall	DitCh	45
12	textURe	frAMe	RefUrnish	44
13	fLAtness	inteRview	UnBuckled	43
14	mechaNIsms	rigId	buNkhouse	42
15	uNendiNg	fratErnal	coNferenCes	41
16	pROceeds	viewpOinT	AmbitiouS	40
17	incluSiVe	proJectOr	marRied	39
18	avalanChE	FormS	keenNess	38
19	mArroW	diScoloR	ExpIring	37
20	sieMens	unchAngEd	repubLIcans	36
21	instrumeNTs	MItchell	CompOund	35
22	EValuation	assuMptiOn	monoLOgue	34
23	DesigNate	alloCaTion	sloVakIa	33
24	cArOlina	diSplayS	deFlAtor	32
25	GrIef	reclUsiVe	monumEnt	31
26	skiLl	hunGAry	AqUatic	30
	27	28	29	

	58	57	56	
1	supportIng	compriSEd	Translate	55
2	JitTers	williamS	PrUne	54
3	plEntifUl	PriorIty	Retrain	53
4	uncLaImed	BoroUgh	vAcatE	52
5	SaucinesS	uNmasked	prEseasoN	51
6	expertise	ampLiFier	chOkeHold	50
7	Progeny	resPect	FUnded	49
8	snoWdrifT	CaribbeAn	grImY	48
9	standarDS	OccultisT	eNforcemenT	47
10	empLOyees	loNgesT	aPpropRiate	46
11	activIties	KatRina	StarK	45
12	arcHivE	bONfire	prOprieTary	44
13	rElatIng	cONsumption	heaDerS	43
14	swimsuiT	eXcusaBle	tRains	42
15	underStOod	UniversaL	meXiCo	41
16	ilLnEss	moDUlar	overspenD	40
17	coMparisoN	paramEters	cliMbIng	39
18	straTegies	CarryinG	RecordeRs	38
19	ExpertiSe	blAbbeR	Glenn	37
20	RefUnd	graffiTI	oBServed	36
21	dUmpLing	preAchy	fUturE	35
22	CranberrY	tradeMaRks	faceLifT	34
23	tInkliNg	playiNG	DreamBoat	33
24	Disposal	SafAri	wOrrieD	32
25	cHemiSt	HeavIng	TighTrope	31
26	mAnhandLe	unvaLUed	seAfooD	30
	27	28	29	

	58	57	56	
1	GlasgoW	ManchesteR	espResso	55
2	bAckdrOp	AsIde	LukewarM	54
3	ResEller	flavoRFul	conteNd	53
4	ChRistian	reunitE	OmEga	52
5	sHakirA	weIghtS	replaCed	51
6	suspEctEd	IslAm	sTAges	50
7	coordiNaTed	conNEctor	enJOying	49
8	iNvitations	patriOt	sECular	48
9	cRitiCal	Budapest	THong	47
10	unrulY	recOveRy	powdEreD	46
11	CrUnchy	originAlLy	uNcoRk	45
12	neUtrAl	unRulY	brYan	44
13	PAvilion	monoTone	GrIme	43
14	AuditiOn	fillED	baCklighT	42
15	ExAlted	Divisive	ActivAted	41
16	TunIng	sTevenS	astronOmy	40
17	waLnUt	MOrris	drEambOat	39
18	senSitize	sySteMatic	gratuIT	38
19	tigreSS	cusToms	frigIditY	37
20	SAlem	cOmPel	laTesT	36
21	catFish	imPliciT	uncUreD	35
22	negLigenT	coNsulTants	SHooting	34
23	comPacter	pRacticEs	glutInous	33
24	previoUS	BelOng	actually	32
25	JIngle	haZaRd	coLlaR	31
26	Awning	viEWed	distReSs	30
	27	28	29	

	58	57	56	
1	smooth	ChattEr	chlorIdE	55
2	Inspection	spiNacH	amiSs	54
3	dislIkiNg	merCedEs	uNcloAk	53
4	fesTEr	aGaiNst	TRies	52
5	sTuMble	CooRdinates	defiNitionS	51
6	ReSidents	singLEs	HalLoween	50
7	IdiOm	wRongeD	stylishLY	49
8	inHeriTed	NaVigate	maRblE	48
9	wideLy	unseemly	Herein	47
10	aSsessiNg	ReattaCh	DefRaud	46
11	pegbOard	Impact	pUshovEr	45
12	eNriCh	Purposes	cHasE	44
13	SAndpaper	opOssum	CommuNities	43
14	studYiNg	rePresenTs	cLeAred	42
15	Shown	germiNate	GambliNg	41
16	ripEniNg	likeLihooD	unRolL	40
17	headfiRsT	excHange	anYtHing	39
18	dAndy	uNdRilled	ACcompany	38
19	comPoseR	asSesSed	rePeatEr	37
20	TooLbar	ENdurable	writers	36
21	kiNshiP	coTton	MummiFy	35
22	Uniform	statIC	habItaNt	34
23	buyers	BreathiNg	tOngUe	33
24	Green	anoNymoUs	BriefS	32
25	baggAgE	hanDpIck	promIsE	31
26	doorsTOp	AmeniTies	freQuenCy	30
	27	28	29	

	58	57	56	
1	coNstraIn	aMbienT	ObstRuct	55
2	caNdY	explainED	eNhanciNg	54
3	FedEral	houSewarEs	SpeakIng	53
4	elEctricitY	SupErman	footsie	52
5	rEaRrange	refINish	GardenS	51
6	ameRIcans	begInNers	FloridA	50
7	chrIstiaNs	PersonalLy	deFroSt	49
8	sentENces	RiddanCe	percEntAge	48
9	seaSonAl	AngEl	AccompaNy	47
10	sUblevEl	ninth	TreSpass	46
11	objEctives	meaNT	BreAst	45
12	perfEcTly	drIzzLe	EnclOse	44
13	snazzy	coMpromIse	VietnaM	43
14	corrEction	mobiLEs	escapable	42
15	bUlLpen	treAT	mItchell	41
16	AmusinG	aFfeCted	chEWy	40
17	compLetiOn	freeWaRe	proJectOrs	39
18	nicOtinE	aLcohoL	boOty	38
19	CItations	festIvAls	mEmphIs	37
20	sEparateD	fLAtly	cOverinG	36
21	BOundless	InformaTive	opeRa	35
22	symposium	pAssAble	cOmmencE	34
23	HardneSs	detenTioN	geNEral	33
24	deLegAtion	roBbIng	reSidentiaL	32
25	foUntaIn	efficienCy	preliminARy	31
26	glucOsE	maGnificenT	lAngUages	30
	27	28	29	

	RANDSTR=AVa8aza	PIN=210467	GRID# 8	
	58	57	56	
1	doorsToP	Stage	stuffed	55
2	ReseArch	barBEcue	crescent	54
3	ScAnning	suPpOrt	blOAted	53
4	freeZe	haBitAnt	sTriPes	52
5	CorneLl	maShEd	comMenT	51
6	deSkbouNd	abanDOned	cOnsistEncy	50
7	kleenEx	buddhiSm	practICe	49
8	unlEvelEd	mOnsoon	thUmbnaiLs	48
9	baLcOny	aPpraisAl	nePaL	47
10	cushy	UnbuCkled	staGIng	46
11	moaNIng	BabBle	pRIor	45
12	paRtridGe	prImary	atmospherE	44
13	stacK	empathiC	orDiNance	43
14	uNnAmable	endoRsemenT	sExuaLity	42
15	bounDaries	urUgUay	nAtIon	41
16	untwist	REsorts	obLigatIons	40
17	blOGger	StRay	buNioN	39
18	Squeamish	vITalize	Colonist	38
19	osmOSis	amPLify	Chair	37
20	mothBalL	trEkker	hAsTe	36
21	seVEnteen	refriED	coolEr	35
22	retReAt	unfocuSEd	recTangLe	34
23	woRldwIde	poRtIons	clumSIly	33
24	iNtrAnet	JigsAw	EasTern	32
25	cAring	Lecturer	supPorTed	31
26	tElesCope	sPeakErs	HighS	30
	27	28	29	

	58	57	56	
1	opERate	fOotgEar	DestructIon	55
2	handsaW	spranG	ReCycling	54
3	theIr	mORbidity	UnKnowing	53
4	maRkers	exhibit	coNventions	52
5	experImenTs	ChEwable	wheel	51
6	syRiA	Licensed	overnIght	50
7	elusiVe	frEelancE	pAlestiniaN	49
8	ouTMatch	fastEst	UnsAfe	48
9	Element	caDmiuM	deStRuct	47
10	HandyMan	portRaIt	campaiGns	46
11	IndIcator	enGagiNg	ScreenshOts	45
12	kindneSs	unpaiD	Trace	44
13	slidesHow	GratiS	Chummy	43
14	pArtrIdge	maNhandlE	TWeezers	42
15	DisiNfect	liMElight	Zones	41
16	CurfeW	utiLitieS	neithER	40
17	volatILe	approxiMaTe	AbsoLve	39
18	DiffusIve	viVaCious	reaTTach	38
19	nONprofit	sleEpinG	wHisKing	37
20	banIstEr	RIgid	greAter	36
21	bounCiNg	ScaRy	FootbOard	35
22	mcDonald	UntaggEd	meASuring	34
23	iMpoTence	esTeemEd	occupiEd	33
24	tIFfany	cordlesS	outbUrst	32
25	pUrebrEd	fRiDay	anywHere	31
26	soLuTions	ongOIng	deVotEe	30
	27	28	29	

	RANDSTR=n)hHFh7	PIN=706913	GRID# 10	
	58	57	56	
1	coUples	hEavEn	TrusTable	55
2	deLegatE	manNeD	rEadiNgs	54
3	ReacH	sYnDicate	DevelopeRs	53
4	imPurE	icElaNd	uNdYing	52
5	WorkStation	flashbacK	prEformEd	51
6	opeRatiVe	cHaLlenge	vErtiCal	50
7	HanDclasp	prESs	Darkened	49
8	inteREsts	HamPshire	oVeRlay	48
9	restauranT	astRonaut	faNciEd	47
10	concEal	sHePherd	Views	46
11	Hypocrite	iNdEx	flyablE	45
12	TWine	clIcks	pOlIcy	44
13	dEltA	HerBal	OfflinE	43
14	trillIon	scOunDrel	chAnCes	42
15	groUnDwater	OccUpy	IrreguLar	41
16	foundAtIon	PoSter	dePLoy	40
17	switzErlanD	cLosE	busInEss	39
18	bLing	aLmanac	sPilL	38
19	HierarchY	diploma	encouRagE	37
20	shAding	coMmoNly	dEpressIon	36
21	ManNer	JasminE	Amnesty	35
22	cOncluDed	CorporatiOn	suPErvisors	34
23	trilliOn	terrAcE	BakesHop	33
24	epidERmal	microsOfT	germinate	32
25	jArgon	grunGE	bodIEs	31
26	tableware	properTIes	sHeriff	30
	27	28	29	

	58	57	56	
1	cAThedral	beDRooms	repulSiVe	55
2	Prenatal	exposeD	FIelds	54
3	StaTistic	migraTioN	SmaRtness	53
4	reemerGE	taMeNess	NichOlas	52
5	moNaCo	scOotEr	iNtensity	51
6	conDucted	abStracT	bartEndEr	50
7	TWeezers	eggpLanT	bReak	49
8	healiNG	bOulevArd	BarmAid	48
9	ProZac	preFormed	ThwartinG	47
10	SEdative	reaTtach	taggEd	46
11	ProVisions	exorcISt	bRitAnnica	45
12	trIfocalS	downloaded	auThentic	44
13	chAIrs	comparablE	uNdRess	43
14	workflOw	unclAmPed	uNdiVided	42
15	sandFIsh	sTaTe	variatiOns	41
16	diNner	UnpaDded	backiNg	40
17	unLuckiLy	Triple	telesCOpe	39
18	unfeeliNg	chOrUs	upsTreaM	38
19	dEpartmentS	biNDing	cArEer	37
20	afteRmAth	retAinEr	acCreDited	36
21	fesTeR	traNQuil	speciFic	35
22	scientiST	instRucTion	collIsioN	34
23	NurSing	unbaLAnce	deViCes	33
24	ouTdOors	sCorN	Absurd	32
25	BackshifT	reptilIAn	iSolatinG	31
26	huNtIngton	VeRbally	musicaL	30
	27	28	29	

	RANDSTR=#iP,[dK	PIN=715537	GRID# 12	
	58	57	56	
1	JerrY	mentIonEd	awaRdeD	55
2	diNginEss	GraduatioN	AfGhanistan	54
3	blooMing	uPFront	evIdeNt	53
4	prAnkstEr	terriBlE	errANt	52
5	nastinESs	SupeRvisors	DenoTe	51
6	blOcked	consisting	unbeNd	50
7	liNgO	MorphiNe	rubdowN	49
8	eLectRon	conTractoR	guESt	48
9	flashback	coMBat	tWice	47
10	scaNNer	UnbiTten	cOnvergencE	46
11	moNoRail	MoniTors	eNGine	45
12	MadagascaR	afteRgloW	bAtteRed	44
13	cinciNnaTi	meMOrabilia	conducTinG	43
14	legenD	pyRaMid	suStaineR	42
15	RegulateD	actiVist	DeNtist	41
16	clinIc	suRreal	riDEs	40
17	unceRtaintY	siNgleS	malpracTiCe	39
18	ReporteR	disabILity	retaIneR	38
19	fLatwoRm	ChowdeR	bUildIng	37
20	Repaying	handBaGs	incomiNG	36
21	sTatemEnts	reviVaBle	oblivIOn	35
22	faBlE	annuaLlY	devElopeD	34
23	anyHow	hEmstItch	marBling	33
24	britAiN	MicHelle	ImprOved	32
25	slaShing	welcOmE	UselesslY	31
26	richnesS	iNvision	ConcepT	30
	27	28	29	

RANDSTR=N-$,+G2   PIN=722041   GRID# 13

	58	57	56	
1	scarecROw	friVolous	cOgnitiVe	55
2	disfIguRe	uNawAre	activIsTs	54
3	clEaNer	treAtmenTs	TaMil	53
4	cRudeness	sLingiNg	caLlEd	52
5	EquivalEnt	vocabUlary	spiritISm	51
6	fInAlize	pRocuremEnt	cHiLdrens	50
7	poRSche	daffodiL	hurrIEd	49
8	UpLifted	composT	uNcoileD	48
9	ReGulator	retUrnEd	HUskiness	47
10	constituTE	riDers	LArry	46
11	conVenience	musHinesS	ElEctric	45
12	HUndred	HiltoN	consideRing	44
13	unhealtHY	matteRS	holdinGS	43
14	SadDen	TrackbacKs	chOlEsterol	42
15	hospItAlity	diSCover	FOllicle	41
16	cRaNium	BaMboo	sunglaSses	40
17	DangeR	incomPleTe	LaboraTory	39
18	proDuCtions	ShOrthand	GraceleSs	38
19	inveST	progRamming	DeclaratiOn	37
20	CognItion	overUse	queenSlanD	36
21	presEnts	taCTics	direCtory	35
22	haPPily	condiTionAl	Repulsive	34
23	camcorDeR	LUridness	italicize	33
24	shiVerinG	reGaRded	gLaDiator	32
25	shoWGirl	stUdyIng	straddLe	31
26	lethaRgY	tIMes	deGrees	30
	27	28	29	

	58	57	56	
1	somEBody	temporarIlY	purgatOry	55
2	socCEr	dEferraL	quoTeS	54
3	unlOvablE	SpeArfish	gEranIum	53
4	eNglAnd	emphATic	Individuals	52
5	valUables	HandLer	explAineD	51
6	unleArned	ExclusiOn	ferrARi	50
7	StroNgman	shakira	InteRior	49
8	catHouSe	unwoManly	uNblessEd	48
9	soMetiMes	RaNger	PsychiAtry	47
10	braZil	rEtainEd	patchWorK	46
11	oLympUs	solUtiOn	eRasuRe	45
12	progRaMme	NIgeria	muSeuMs	44
13	hUngrY	RecommenDed	NormAl	43
14	translateD	bazoOkA	prEdefIne	42
15	infLuEnces	owNeRship	compOunD	41
16	iMpart	eMploYees	haNdBall	40
17	CrinkLy	decEmBer	uninjUred	39
18	specifies	BEginners	tYcooN	38
19	uNholy	uninvIted	fRantic	37
20	especIallY	SaxOphone	shIpmeNt	36
21	SwImwear	louIsiAna	exCellenCe	35
22	bAnnisTer	caLIbrate	wildlife	34
23	anTarcTica	dUckling	amBaSsador	33
24	reCapture	SamSung	uNliMited	32
25	roNAld	spLAshed	reuNIte	31
26	SanDing	Sandbar	expEnsiVe	30
	27	28	29	

	58	57	56	
1	EdiTorials	ensuRE	outselL	55
2	UnEnvied	assigNmeNts	anEMia	54
3	lAndownEr	shoPS	jawliNe	53
4	atMosPheric	samsuNG	uNfounDed	52
5	keywoRdS	custoMarY	AthletIcs	51
6	coMpletinG	InsurancE	cOnsists	50
7	purpLE	agoNizE	undeRstooD	49
8	ducKtAil	veGetAtion	vOtEr	48
9	attractIvE	rElAxation	energeTiC	47
10	sUnglasSes	swiTChes	demyStify	46
11	During	lEcTure	WhisKing	45
12	HiriNg	AmbassaDor	SticK	44
13	UnguardeD	pRinceTon	sPlashy	43
14	lEgroOm	applicaTioN	flashIlY	42
15	pestIcide	pErfecTly	compActEr	41
16	rUbblE	EdgAr	profEssor	40
17	DiaBolic	rAkinG	easTcOast	39
18	juJiTsu	cOnsideRing	hosteD	38
19	pAydAy	lOOksmart	cobblEr	37
20	uNeThical	spIeD	sTernneSs	36
21	ProFessed	ArroGant	prEpPy	35
22	profesSion	paddEd	specuLaTe	34
23	broadWAy	steeRsmAn	gRudgiNg	33
24	TreachEry	Conical	TRansit	32
25	develOPed	REnter	harMonics	31
26	draiNabLe	thonGS	agonizing	30
	27	28	29	

	58	57	56	
1	asToUnd	creaTiOn	arGUment	55
2	uNdoIng	sTraIned	reSpOndents	54
3	reToOl	Smithsonian	driNking	53
4	RavIne	SmoldEr	poWer	52
5	SyMbols	ConceRned	Admin	51
6	confIGure	underdOnE	orDiNance	50
7	sIlenCer	aUDit	tiptoeiNg	49
8	leXmark	repROach	MedlIne	48
9	absEntEe	ProgrammeR	smokEleSs	47
10	decEmbeR	darkenEd	FlatnEss	46
11	fOndneSs	tsunaMi	FlaShing	45
12	TwEezers	MiNing	clEAver	44
13	ridEr	cooKIe	straTegies	43
14	stoCKings	eLectoraL	trUsteE	42
15	overstoCK	SwiFt	legwOrK	41
16	cuStomers	wIKipedia	recommenDeD	40
17	retaininG	LeonaRd	buCKwheat	39
18	mEmbeR	iSsUing	vOlkswageN	38
19	schematIc	earnINg	kijiJI	37
20	swadDling	conTainiNg	transActIon	36
21	hampsHiRe	uTmost	divISions	35
22	lOttery	BrAve	glOsS	34
23	SteadyiNg	NEarness	reViveR	33
24	QUalifier	FiliNg	subSCript	32
25	GLance	MadonNa	struct	31
26	OperatIonal	aFter	quOte	30
	27	28	29	

	58	57	56	
1	thinGS	TigerS	AlertS	55
2	dEsirablE	FeistY	ColumNs	54
3	dIstinctiOn	uNrated	affIliateS	53
4	jusTly	KindlIng	ConfounD	52
5	jUstin	treasURes	wRanGle	51
6	deLayEd	UnfasTen	dEXterous	50
7	undErhanD	dirEctiOns	tWistabLe	49
8	evaluAtIon	ProPose	FitTed	48
9	straTegiC	wOrshipEr	bLend	47
10	hastinEss	danGeroUs	spearhEad	46
11	wEekend	oklahoMa	householD	45
12	catfighT	OutrIght	dilIGent	44
13	sNowbIrd	trapeZoiD	PRograms	43
14	instrUmeNts	gEologIc	peRfecTly	42
15	detecTIve	correlaTIon	toshIbA	41
16	PampeRer	appLIcant	hEnCe	40
17	vEnUs	assigNeD	opaciTy	39
18	irRiGate	alBErt	CoMmence	38
19	bUsily	suNrise	himSeLf	37
20	scaNninG	tunIng	overcOaT	36
21	obtAininG	genERous	heAviLy	35
22	sECrets	tHErefore	LouiS	34
23	bloWIng	uNcoAted	RemovablE	33
24	wrAng@Le	eXperimEnts	AlkalIne	32
25	proacTivE	cleriCaL	stYlisH	31
26	actIviTies	capabilITy	summaRies	30
	27	28	29	

	RANDSTR=FtPE&g.	PIN=221228	GRID# 18	
	58	57	56	
1	GuaraNtee	dAteS	dynamICs	55
2	spiEd	CulminatE	cAmpsiTe	54
3	aspaRAgus	CouRse	dAvidson	53
4	pRovOlone	direcToRs	PyramiD	52
5	housEhOld	musTard	UNpinned	51
6	airport	kuDOs	tUEsday	50
7	instrumeNts	televisioNs	transpiRE	49
8	designerS	directLY	CounTer	48
9	twEEt	unMoveD	emBatTled	47
10	hAmPshire	doMeLike	broKer	46
11	allow	grAdIng	squeAlinG	45
12	cLouD	grUdgIng	bUBbling	44
13	outlOoK	GivEn	readiNGs	43
14	AcceptAble	fidgeTy	CrEates	42
15	risINg	dedicATed	eXcelleNce	41
16	cesArEan	innovaTIon	confLiCts	40
17	disclaimErs	coNSecutive	emBezzLe	39
18	unDertaKe	gReeter	tUrmoil	38
19	greaTeR	inFrAred	venEerinG	37
20	prOtotype	aneMIc	vbUlletin	36
21	tribeSmAn	Nugget	discUsses	35
22	SqUiggle	zIpfIle	TheatRics	34
23	illiNois	coMpactLy	CloseSt	33
24	OverLoad	CalcUlation	niGHts	32
25	psYcHology	scienTist	hAlifax	31
26	stimulUS	excEedIng	AtTractor	30
	27	28	29	

	58	57	56	
1	icelAnD	ReligiOns	incIdEnce	55
2	FRuit	heAdBoard	seCRecy	54
3	Remission	smIliNgly	pLatyPus	53
4	tItles	StevEns	letteRs	52
5	invisibLE	juGgliNg	prunE	51
6	finisHEr	victOr	aNnotate	50
7	cHaRitable	fantaStIc	hEathEr	49
8	ViSible	inStiTution	uploaDEd	48
9	antArctIca	deUtscH	reLatives	47
10	MeaningfUl	uNDerdog	BUrke	46
11	mIdlAnds	buCkTooth	sLIceable	45
12	eLliott	reFLects	deceNt	44
13	sYDney	suRfAcing	PlaNes	43
14	trifLe	siMPsons	showPlaCe	42
15	FinleSs	ecceNtric	rEnder	41
16	sadDen	plAythiNg	unArmorEd	40
17	InstallEd	ArChitects	alReAdy	39
18	HigHer	adVantage	soUlS	38
19	pLayroOm	mAjOrity	PatrOnage	37
20	cOmParing	dIrectIon	iNGredients	36
21	Outreach	jiNGle	RusSian	35
22	sMudGy	JunKman	merchAnt	34
23	leVerage	AustraliA	profOuNd	33
24	tRainer	ipHone	rEprimaNd	32
25	messaGing	sEcondary	metALlic	31
26	corRuptioN	roUGe	perceiveD	30
	27	28	29	

	RANDSTR=;G]q)xl	PIN=458362	GRID# 20	
	58	57	56	
1	algoriThm	SadlY	ashEn	55
2	BUyers	essentIal	mexICo	54
3	useLEssly	ProcEdure	bannIsteR	53
4	conducIvE	hUmOrless	bLAtantly	52
5	CandY	achIeVed	sPecIalized	51
6	nasTily	diffusioN	unrivaleD	50
7	maLfoRmed	heAdBoard	suBtotal	49
8	LicensE	milWaUkee	cuiSiNe	48
9	taught	tItaniuM	Stroke	47
10	imperiaL	excLudiNg	prodUcE	46
11	PostS	gloSs	stRuggLe	45
12	demeAnIng	ouTplayeD	cRown	44
13	bEnnett	preFereNces	oxidiziNg	43
14	sInuoUs	AccepTs	distaStE	42
15	questiONs	SOlar	caLendars	41
16	midLAnds	dEPendent	accordaNce	40
17	nICholas	bAnIster	risOtto	39
18	invasIOn	wIkipedIa	palPablE	38
19	ParTicular	peRFume	baCkpedaL	37
20	awNing	handBAgs	uNtie	36
21	cartridge	OXford	skiMmer	35
22	stRing	ComParison	definItion	34
23	casket	siSTer	caTtaIl	33
24	rEmEdial	RippliNg	battleFieLd	32
25	Character	QueriEs	CaptaiN	31
26	anAlyTical	ScoTland	caTchAble	30
	27	28	29	

67

	58	57	56	
1	beLTs	DainTily	unDerling	55
2	yUgOslavia	peeRs	faStesT	54
3	oVerSleep	plAsmA	wRIters	53
4	siDes	hardeNEd	BeAns	52
5	prEface	DebAting	attendANt	51
6	strolLEr	Ellis	oVercOat	50
7	sTufF	Ronald	SchemIng	49
8	fACtoid	relapsing	goiNg	48
9	cOopEr	obituariES	FeelinG	47
10	viRtUal	HaraSsment	Rockfish	46
11	Allen	bRokeR	InstruCtor	45
12	DesignaTion	LinguIst	matchless	44
13	maCintosh	vengefuL	lightER	43
14	viLlages	maNnIsh	litEracy	42
15	LegislaTive	sUrvivorS	ouTdaTed	41
16	AwaRded	install	sPrUce	40
17	mOrphIng	inSpiratiOn	sCripting	39
18	AcrOnym	amenDabLe	imPRessive	38
19	PEdigree	vIolatioN	reliabiliTY	37
20	HomelAnd	UnriPe	expensIVe	36
21	coRNed	BAcklit	expansiVe	35
22	stIpenD	CubiCle	oppoSite	34
23	EndangEred	rEVersion	drEadlock	33
24	uniforMlY	arranGemeNt	fLeshEd	32
25	nOrton	miRrorS	prOmOtional	31
26	WOozy	corNbaLl	blANdness	30
	27	28	29	

	RANDSTR=UAkUpuk	PIN=768409	GRID# 22	
	58	57	56	
1	rockinESs	mutAtIon	naStilY	55
2	tEenage	RhymE	Communist	54
3	PreSsed	yearniNG	CounCil	53
4	bARcode	reMindFul	uncounTeD	52
5	unfAiR	dancIng	reAbsorB	51
6	grAcefuL	mongOLia	twistabLe	50
7	Condition	seEkinG	BonEy	49
8	wherever	vOterS	bootLeG	48
9	undeRdOg	botCh	buLldOg	47
10	iLlnesS	BehaLf	sUbsiding	46
11	scofF	mOnEtize	maTchiNg	45
12	AdvocacY	clUbS	negAtivE	44
13	oVerblowN	SeCtors	accePtAble	43
14	cLAssics	christOPher	partnErshIp	42
15	tRIps	overBOok	AgeNts	41
16	addresseS	DeliriOus	sMokEless	40
17	paTienCe	enGines	milwaukEE	39
18	ouTnuMber	cooRdInate	dranK	38
19	enlargE	defensIVe	belTS	37
20	chanceLloR	uNranked	dAtabaSes	36
21	cluMsily	conGeSted	hunTSman	35
22	coMmunicate	otheRS	OverheAt	34
23	twiddLiNg	JinGle	perSuAded	33
24	chRistine	negate	junkyard	32
25	snaGged	corNsTalk	objectIve	31
26	rochEsteR	CondO	duckY	30
	27	28	29	

69

	58	57	56	
1	SpiRits	braDLey	requeSting	55
2	habitAT	DenturE	wiLdly	54
3	madness	cOlLective	PrancIng	53
4	cLubBed	delEte	dOminaNt	52
5	judicIAl	taGgeD	scaNning	51
6	handHelD	CoPing	suiTaBle	50
7	sEntence	NinetietH	seCurely	49
8	HospitaLity	divIders	desIgnEr	48
9	resolutioNS	hardENer	integrity	47
10	moOnlighT	reMaRry	coNsensus	46
11	aSiDe	aFghaNistan	landside	45
12	unsToppEd	rEvereD	raPIdly	44
13	pLatyPus	conceDEd	gENerous	43
14	reSPonse	DrizZle	arthRitIs	42
15	Western	rifliNG	Sweet	41
16	Transexual	kilowatt	crOoN	40
17	Hearings	amazingly	plEthoRa	39
18	TucKing	riVErbed	scUlptoR	38
19	DaVidson	wreckEr	tuRnS	37
20	ImaginaTion	sCaRed	VerbalLy	36
21	insuLIn	unlOckIng	ConfIgure	35
22	cArefuL	diSTort	antIviral	34
23	foRGet	LendErs	tokeN	33
24	frivOlous	tRAcing	gEraniUm	32
25	rEductIon	trout	pAnIc	31
26	cOmpetitIve	squUigGly	strainED	30
	27	28	29	

70

	RANDSTR=$HgKUwP	PIN=521377	GRID# 24	
	58	57	56	
1	fuRniTure	keYworDs	cOntrol	55
2	pEnetRation	mAgneTic	dayTOn	54
3	dIzzIness	colleagues	shadEd	53
4	culPrit	convInced	ReceiVe	52
5	hyPoCrite	premIum	unDerwear	51
6	eXpeDiter	ImPact	utiliTIes	50
7	sAppinEss	eUrOpe	Allocated	49
8	pOssiblY	ovErheaR	BackpedAl	48
9	RetriAl	catliKe	flagshiP	47
10	riverbAnK	antAciD	jaYwaLker	46
11	grilL	Scorebook	betTiNg	45
12	PittsbuRgh	traVElling	obTaining	44
13	enviAbly	strict	bullSeyE	43
14	spoilIng	DebIt	craFTs	42
15	pracTiceS	hURling	doUche	41
16	andReas	GuestboOk	soMeonE	40
17	garciA	anatoMIst	eNableD	39
18	dEvoTee	wolveRiNe	wAvinesS	38
19	mAhoganY	EmphasIze	traitOR	37
20	constrICt	enForcer	PlentIful	36
21	quEstions	cOstUmes	SportS	35
22	dried	ExpiriNg	mOntgomery	34
23	speCIally	staRtle	gArAge	33
24	ResistAnt	cOsmeticS	rEfurBished	32
25	ThIeving	prEorder	rOamIng	31
26	wobblY	sociologY	IncHes	30
	27	28	29	

	58	57	56	
1	hydrocOdone	Nurses	StrudeL	55
2	lOcAtion	gluttON	squishIEr	54
3	regreTFul	FidgeTing	DuckbIll	53
4	MuTate	sErverS	eNlargemenT	52
5	ChEat	Therefore	RiPening	51
6	NaSty	Exquisite	twentiEtH	50
7	uNdercoAt	offeRinG	diamOndS	49
8	motEls	public	SteadieR	48
9	intErracIal	uNcuRious	charger	47
10	provisiON	ConsOnant	Coleman	46
11	lAndScapes	AstronauT	lawyErS	45
12	BloGging	saNdstorM	DiscLaimers	44
13	OutrAnk	pReachEr	coTtaGes	43
14	corPoRation	gibRaltAr	volksWageN	42
15	cliNic	mounted	stRategIes	41
16	DIfficult	techNicIan	banKNote	40
17	usErS	wEbpagE	vAcancIes	39
18	thIckNess	squabBlE	swAddlinG	38
19	PhOnebook	EthanOl	specifIC	37
20	BElarus	missOUri	faciliTate	36
21	labradoR	unliKabLe	combinAtiOn	35
22	doLpHin	PitTsburgh	nOrmaL	34
23	hOmetoWn	ebOok	uneaSily	33
24	anTennaE	latinaS	orGanizIng	32
25	pEnguIn	median	rAvIoli	31
26	DEsignation	medLinE	cloSing	30
	27	28	29	

	58	57	56	
1	hANdwoven	frAnkfUrt	DoorkNob	55
2	hAtlEss	Figment	criTerIon	54
3	ReveaLs	qUartErly	maNcHester	53
4	sirEN	scannER	prOteiNs	52
5	thErapY	resisTAnt	lEgAlly	51
6	sugGestS	cartOOn	divinity	50
7	gibbeRiSh	snOwfLake	vErtEx	49
8	Monica	peRmiTs	chroNIcle	48
9	pHenomenoN	unfuNdEd	gibSOn	47
10	unLeAded	ShakY	lAtEly	46
11	enTRench	ouTlook	ModiFy	45
12	moDeratE	lEWis	flaShiNg	44
13	mONorail	syntheTic	LauncheS	43
14	swazIlaNd	artisTic	dayliGHt	42
15	convIctiOn	ProgrEssive	specIAlists	41
16	jarriNg	oUTcast	uNNoticed	40
17	bOnds	poIntlEss	attraCtOr	39
18	infOrMative	labElEd	coNvEnient	38
19	DivOrcee	tiCkEt	eNcrusT	37
20	TigHt	prActicAl	modiFy	36
21	conclusIonS	deValue	micrOwavE	35
22	CurrentLy	VividnEss	swIpe	34
23	revIewIng	CirCling	tremblinG	33
24	adjust	marrIeD	adaptive	32
25	LegisLate	VamPire	TuLip	31
26	PlEasant	agonIzing	rePorter	30
	27	28	29	

	58	57	56	
1	emptY	holdiNGs	headSmAn	55
2	antiQuely	pERsonally	AmeNdment	54
3	sOmetimEs	bABied	method	53
4	pETted	backed	buCkshoT	52
5	gatheREd	muShiLy	phonebOok	51
6	taBlewAre	prOPerly	iSotOpe	50
7	EvaluAtions	cOmposiTion	paRalLel	49
8	denIEd	HuntsmAn	yelLOw	48
9	AmenDments	Nickel	webpaGE	47
10	ballET	temPorarIly	sEcurities	46
11	unVoCal	desiGneR	BaCktalk	45
12	Adaptation	OfferinG	CourSe	44
13	pixelS	reCeIvers	StriKing	43
14	rEpayinG	freebiE	appraiSAl	42
15	sceNaRios	RisiNg	SearCh	41
16	doOrs	Worlds	surFacing	40
17	unlAcEd	sOluTion	rhYMe	39
18	pErIpheral	jOkinGly	exhibiTioN	38
19	sUddeNly	ArmEd	sofTwaRe	37
20	cReates	BrotheRs	BAsically	36
21	Gallon	pamELa	minus	35
22	orchestrA	intEgrating	pReliminarY	34
23	SinGh	SeLection	DisputE	33
24	rEocCupy	deVouTly	RicHardson	32
25	theRaPeutic	inSerted	postposTeD	31
26	CRiticism	cONcern	varIety	30
	27	28	29	

	RANDSTR=D+gn7DE	PIN=078532	GRID# 28	
	58	57	56	
1	peTtinesS	assesSmeNt	softwArE	55
2	culmiNAte	doMinoEs	absentEe	54
3	REnegade	hypnOseS	percEptioN	53
4	frEedoM	eXpeNse	combinatIOn	52
5	DutiEs	oXFord	qUarTers	51
6	cOmplAints	manchESter	RetrIeved	50
7	unmatcHeD	AlmiGhty	peRMissions	49
8	ratio	micrOsOft	moLecUle	48
9	unExpEcted	tAbleWare	ReBate	47
10	seAtTle	mathEmAtics	cartooN	46
11	DragoniSh	harRison	obViOus	45
12	gravITy	IriSh	tunIsIa	44
13	POsters	bLeeP	mEdiCation	43
14	eMotion	sOUls	nuMerAl	42
15	DrAwing	ImpulsE	ImpotenT	41
16	hArdcorE	phillIps	exprEssioN	40
17	DeFendant	anTSy	oBseSsion	39
18	zshoPS	oFFline	pReteXt	38
19	pioNeeR	MotOcross	leverS	37
20	encrOaCh	EdGes	EGgplant	36
21	deTeNtion	mexiCAn	projecTIon	35
22	paviLion	uncoMmOn	actUallY	34
23	pREcious	PuzzlIng	jAwlEss	33
24	frActiOn	BLitz	Strategic	32
25	legItimAte	wobBly	gLoVe	31
26	TArgets	RelaTing	sciENce	30
	27	28	29	

75

	58	57	56	
1	hapPiNess	corrAl	sTripS	55
2	arraNgeD	freCkled	nurserY	54
3	horiZOntal	headAChe	enterINg	53
4	accePtAble	aSSure	trUMp	52
5	PopPy	goveRninG	unsubsCribe	51
6	indUstrIal	friSbeE	SpiNster	50
7	furNIshed	colLEctor	clavIclE	49
8	fOotHold	uPDated	sANctuary	48
9	veRbalize	upRoar	enlArGement	47
10	femInism	bUlLseye	pRoVinces	46
11	doRmitory	daintIly	disCoverEd	45
12	trInidAd	grApplE	ScrunCh	44
13	matrimoNY	mUsicians	beacHeS	43
14	indIcate	uNshEathe	fIgurIne	42
15	flankiNG	wOManhood	hUmpbaCk	41
16	unfunDeD	reviseD	togetHer	40
17	betTeR	refUSed	shEEp	39
18	persONally	remoViNg	reproceSs	38
19	rUmblIng	cahOots	rOckIng	37
20	exCusabLy	atTendanCe	mOaniNg	36
21	bOoTh	imPortanTly	oXidizing	35
22	ExteNsive	cavaLIer	evaLuations	34
23	fairfIeld	thEsE	schOlarship	33
24	rippLe	habITual	perfeCtlY	32
25	violatE	permisSioNs	facIal	31
26	mOnica	imPortAnt	NuggEt	30
	27	28	29	

	58	57	56	
1	quARter	reTirement	eMptinEss	55
2	scHemes	graduATed	PrinT	54
3	qUeEns	suBjects	sMokineSs	53
4	reFiNance	daughtEr	plumBIng	52
5	ExpectanT	enCouRages	Knelt	51
6	waGgle	frEqueNcy	mAlfOrmed	50
7	appeALing	TrImmer	numBing	49
8	woRkstaTion	CanoPy	settleMent	48
9	haNDball	glutInoUs	sCouT	47
10	cReatiOns	nebULizer	numeratoR	46
11	juLIe	keroSene	prodUCtions	45
12	wAlleT	muLTiply	malFormeD	44
13	OfferS	wildFire	SLather	43
14	liteRaTure	cosigNEr	sQuattEr	42
15	chaMber	unliKEly	confiNing	41
16	unhAppy	VastlY	rEappoinT	40
17	EvalUator	bAtterEd	siMOn	39
18	upgrAdEs	overCroWd	elEctAble	38
19	DadDy	MoBster	tRibunaL	37
20	UnbUckled	punGenT	suItAbly	36
21	pluMbinG	maRShall	PArting	35
22	lUDicrous	unCErtainty	flashy	34
23	dULler	aMericas	emERgency	33
24	DocUment	SecOnds	dreamlESs	32
25	dooRsTop	Riches	SolaRis	31
26	eNigmAtic	brAcelEt	SUrname	30
	27	28	29	

77

ONLINE ACCOUNTS
& PASSWORDS

Site/Server:

Username:

GridKey:

Password:

Notes:

A

Site/Server:

Username:

GridKey:

Password:

Notes:

A

Site/Server:

Username:

GridKey:

Password:

Notes:

A

Site/Server:

Username:

GridKey:

Password:

Notes:

A

Site/Server:

Username:

GridKey:

Password:

Notes:

A

B

Site/Server:

Username:

GridKey:

Password:

Notes:

B

Site/Server:

Username:

GridKey:

Password:

Notes:

B

Site/Server:

Username:

GridKey:

Password:

Notes:

B

Site/Server:

Username:

GridKey:

Password:

Notes:

B

Site/Server:

Username:

GridKey:

Password:

Notes:

Site/Server:

Username:

GridKey:

Password:

Notes:

C

Site/Server:

Username:

GridKey:

Password:

Notes:

C

Site/Server:

Username:

GridKey:

Password:

Notes:

C

Site/Server:

Username:

GridKey:

Password:

Notes:

C

Site/Server:

Username:

GridKey:

Password:

Notes:

C

D

Site/Server:

Username:

GridKey:

Password:

Notes:

D

Site/Server:

Username:

GridKey:

Password:

Notes:

D

Site/Server:

Username:

GridKey:

Password:

Notes:

D

Site/Server:

Username:

GridKey:

Password:

Notes:

D

Site/Server:

Username:

GridKey:

Password:

Notes:

Site/Server:

Username:

GridKey:

Password:

Notes:

E

Site/Server:

Username:

GridKey:

Password:

Notes:

E

Site/Server:

Username:

GridKey:

Password:

Notes:

E

Site/Server:

Username:

GridKey:

Password:

Notes:

E

Site/Server:

Username:

GridKey:

Password:

Notes:

E

F

Site/Server:

Username:

GridKey:

Password:

Notes:

F

Site/Server:

Username:

GridKey:

Password:

Notes:

F

Site/Server:

Username:

GridKey:

Password:

Notes:

F

Site/Server:

Username:

GridKey:

Password:

Notes:

F

Site/Server:

Username:

GridKey:

Password:

Notes:

Site/Server:

Username:

GridKey:

Password:

Notes:

G

Site/Server:

Username:

GridKey:

Password:

Notes:

G

Site/Server:

Username:

GridKey:

Password:

Notes:

G

Site/Server:

Username:

GridKey:

Password:

Notes:

G

Site/Server:

Username:

GridKey:

Password:

Notes:

G

H

Site/Server:

Username:

GridKey:

Password:

Notes:

H

Site/Server:

Username:

GridKey:

Password:

Notes:

H

Site/Server:

Username:

GridKey:

Password:

Notes:

H

Site/Server:

Username:

GridKey:

Password:

Notes:

H

Site/Server:

Username:

GridKey:

Password:

Notes:

Site/Server:

Username:

GridKey:

Password:

Notes:

Site/Server:

Username:

GridKey:

Password:

Notes:

Site/Server:

Username:

GridKey:

Password:

Notes:

Site/Server:

Username:

GridKey:

Password:

Notes:

Site/Server:

Username:

GridKey:

Password:

Notes:

J

Site/Server:

Username:

GridKey:

Password:

Notes:

J

Site/Server:

Username:

GridKey:

Password:

Notes:

J

Site/Server:

Username:

GridKey:

Password:

Notes:

J

Site/Server:

Username:

GridKey:

Password:

Notes:

J

Site/Server:

Username:

GridKey:

Password:

Notes:

Site/Server:

Username:

GridKey:

Password:

Notes:

K

Site/Server:

Username:

GridKey:

Password:

Notes:

K

Site/Server:

Username:

GridKey:

Password:

Notes:

K

Site/Server:

Username:

GridKey:

Password:

Notes:

K

Site/Server:

Username:

GridKey:

Password:

Notes:

K

L

Site/Server:

Username:

GridKey:

Password:

Notes:

L

Site/Server:

Username:

GridKey:

Password:

Notes:

L

Site/Server:

Username:

GridKey:

Password:

Notes:

L

Site/Server:

Username:

GridKey:

Password:

Notes:

L

Site/Server:

Username:

GridKey:

Password:

Notes:

Site/Server:

Username:

GridKey:

Password:

Notes:

M

Site/Server:

Username:

GridKey:

Password:

Notes:

M

Site/Server:

Username:

GridKey:

Password:

Notes:

M

Site/Server:

Username:

GridKey:

Password:

Notes:

M

Site/Server:

Username:

GridKey:

Password:

Notes:

M

N

Site/Server:

Username:

GridKey:

Password:

Notes:

N

Site/Server:

Username:

GridKey:

Password:

Notes:

N

Site/Server:

Username:

GridKey:

Password:

Notes:

N

Site/Server:

Username:

GridKey:

Password:

Notes:

N

Site/Server:

Username:

GridKey:

Password:

Notes:

Site/Server:

Username:

GridKey:

Password:

Notes:

O

Site/Server:

Username:

GridKey:

Password:

Notes:

O

Site/Server:

Username:

GridKey:

Password:

Notes:

O

Site/Server:

Username:

GridKey:

Password:

Notes:

O

Site/Server:

Username:

GridKey:

Password:

Notes:

O

P

Site/Server:

Username:

GridKey:

Password:

Notes:

P

Site/Server:

Username:

GridKey:

Password:

Notes:

P

Site/Server:

Username:

GridKey:

Password:

Notes:

P

Site/Server:

Username:

GridKey:

Password:

Notes:

P

Site/Server:

Username:

GridKey:

Password:

Notes:

Site/Server:

Username:

GridKey:

Password:

Notes:

Q

Site/Server:

Username:

GridKey:

Password:

Notes:

Q

Site/Server:

Username:

GridKey:

Password:

Notes:

Q

Site/Server:

Username:

GridKey:

Password:

Notes:

Q

Site/Server:

Username:

GridKey:

Password:

Notes:

Q

R

Site/Server:

Username:

GridKey:

Password:

Notes:

R

Site/Server:

Username:

GridKey:

Password:

Notes:

R

Site/Server:

Username:

GridKey:

Password:

Notes:

R

Site/Server:

Username:

GridKey:

Password:

Notes:

R

Site/Server:

Username:

GridKey:

Password:

Notes:

Site/Server:

Username:

GridKey:

Password:

Notes:

S

Site/Server:

Username:

GridKey:

Password:

Notes:

S

Site/Server:

Username:

GridKey:

Password:

Notes:

S

Site/Server:

Username:

GridKey:

Password:

Notes:

S

Site/Server:

Username:

GridKey:

Password:

Notes:

S

T

Site/Server:

Username:

GridKey:

Password:

Notes:

T

Site/Server:

Username:

GridKey:

Password:

Notes:

T

Site/Server:

Username:

GridKey:

Password:

Notes:

T

Site/Server:

Username:

GridKey:

Password:

Notes:

T

Site/Server:

Username:

GridKey:

Password:

Notes:

Site/Server:

Username:

GridKey:

Password:

Notes:

U

Site/Server:

Username:

GridKey:

Password:

Notes:

U

Site/Server:

Username:

GridKey:

Password:

Notes:

U

Site/Server:

Username:

GridKey:

Password:

Notes:

U

Site/Server:

Username:

GridKey:

Password:

Notes:

U

V

Site/Server:

Username:

GridKey:

Password:

Notes:

V

Site/Server:

Username:

GridKey:

Password:

Notes:

V

Site/Server:

Username:

GridKey:

Password:

Notes:

V

Site/Server:

Username:

GridKey:

Password:

Notes:

V

Site/Server:

Username:

GridKey:

Password:

Notes:

Site/Server:

Username:

GridKey:

Password:

Notes:

W

Site/Server:

Username:

GridKey:

Password:

Notes:

W

Site/Server:

Username:

GridKey:

Password:

Notes:

W

Site/Server:

Username:

GridKey:

Password:

Notes:

W

Site/Server:

Username:

GridKey:

Password:

Notes:

W

X
Site/Server:
Username:
GridKey:
Password:
Notes:

X
Site/Server:
Username:
GridKey:
Password:
Notes:

X
Site/Server:
Username:
GridKey:
Password:
Notes:

X
Site/Server:
Username:
GridKey:
Password:
Notes:

X
Site/Server:
Username:
GridKey:
Password:
Notes:

Site/Server:

Username:

GridKey:

Password:

Notes:

Y

Site/Server:

Username:

GridKey:

Password:

Notes:

Y

Site/Server:

Username:

GridKey:

Password:

Notes:

Y

Site/Server:

Username:

GridKey:

Password:

Notes:

Y

Site/Server:

Username:

GridKey:

Password:

Notes:

Y

Z

Site/Server:

Username:

GridKey:

Password:

Notes:

Z

Site/Server:

Username:

GridKey:

Password:

Notes:

Z

Site/Server:

Username:

GridKey:

Password:

Notes:

Z

Site/Server:

Username:

GridKey:

Password:

Notes:

Z

Site/Server:

Username:

GridKey:

Password:

Notes:

ENTERPRISE NETWORK
CREDENTIALS

Site/Server:

Username:

GridKey:

Password:

Notes:

Site/Server:

Username:

GridKey:

Password:

Notes:

Site/Server:

Username:

GridKey:

Password:

Notes:

Site/Server:

Username:

GridKey:

Password:

Notes:

Site/Server:

Username:

GridKey:

Password:

Notes:

Site/Server:

Username:

GridKey:

Password:

Notes:

Site/Server:

Username:

GridKey:

Password:

Notes:

Site/Server:

Username:

GridKey:

Password:

Notes:

Site/Server:

Username:

GridKey:

Password:

Notes:

Site/Server:

Username:

GridKey:

Password:

Notes:

Site/Server:

Username:

GridKey:

Password:

Notes:

Site/Server:

Username:

GridKey:

Password:

Notes:

Site/Server:

Username:

GridKey:

Password:

Notes:

Site/Server:

Username:

GridKey:

Password:

Notes:

Site/Server:

Username:

GridKey:

Password:

Notes:

Site/Server:

Username:

GridKey:

Password:

Notes:

Site/Server:

Username:

GridKey:

Password:

Notes:

Site/Server:

Username:

GridKey:

Password:

Notes:

HOME NETWORK
CREDENTIALS

WIFI

Name (SSID): _____

Key/Password: _____

Encryption: _____

Channel: _____

Notes: _____

ROUTER

IP Address: _____

Username: _____

Password: _____

MAC Address: _____

Notes: _____

WAN

IP Address: _____

Hostname: _____

Gateway: _____

DNS: _____

Notes: _____

SERVER

IP Address: _____

Hostname: _____

Username: _____

Password: _____

Notes: _____

SERVER

IP Address: _____

Hostname: _____

Username: _____

Password: _____

Notes: _____

IP Address: _____ **OTHER**

Hostname: _____

Username: _____

Password: _____

Notes: _____

IP Address: _____ **OTHER**

Hostname: _____

Username: _____

Password: _____

Notes: _____

IP Address: _____ **OTHER**

Hostname: _____

Username: _____

Password: _____

Notes: _____

IP Address: _____ **OTHER**

Hostname: _____

Username: _____

Password: _____

Notes: _____

IP Address: _____ **OTHER**

Hostname: _____

Username: _____

Password: _____

Notes: _____

Printed in Great Britain
by Amazon